Walking

with

Grief

We need to think of ourselves primarily as artists; we need to work as poets and sculptors,
colleagues of the brooding, hovering, indwelling spirit. In any artistic work, the originating
conditions are conceptions that are general visions that are vague, aspirations that are fleeting.
Much of what we value, aspire to, and cherish is ineffable; even if we wanted to, we could not
adequately describe it. The final stop in the creative, artistic presence is letting go,
releasing into the wider community the life which has been formed.
-Maria Harris (1932-2005)

Walking with Grief

A Healing Journey

A collaboration in word & image
by Nanette Geertz & Anne Ierardi

Healthsigns Center, Inc.
408 Main St.
Yarmouthport, MA 02675

Book Design by John L. Moore, M3 Graphic Design

Printed in the United States of America
Library of Congress Control Number: 2005938027
ISBN: 0-9776583-0-9

For the Geertz family

Every painful event contains in itself a seed of growth and liberation.
-Anthony DeMello

Forward

Feelings of loneliness, isolation and depression are familiar to those in mourning.
Especially after the sudden loss of a beloved child, hopelessness and despair
threaten to engulf those who are left behind by extinguishing their will to live.

I can think of no greater resource of comfort and help than *Walking with Grief*.
What a magnificent blending of art and heart- the profoundly insightful poetry
of Nanette Geertz together with the deeply sensitive painting of Anne Ierardi!
Here is a direct line to the bereaved that will gently guide their heartbreak,
encouraging them to live again.

There is no greater spiritual message than one must not run but "walk through the
valley of death" and in the words of the Song of Songs, "Love is stronger than the grave."
This is a book that will be read and reread again and again, offering hope and healing.

Rabbi Earl A. Grollman DHL; DD
Author of *Living When A Loved One Has Died*
and *Straight Talk about Death for Teenagers*

Notes From The Artist

After walking on the boardwalk, overlooking the ocean and marshes at Gray's beach, Nan Geertz
handed me a two page prose poem. She intuited that I would illustrate her poem.

As "spiritual friends", Nan and I had walked together through times of grief, joy, and wonder guided by the
spirit of infinite wisdom. The title of our collaboration, *Walking with Grief* speaks of these walks together
and of Nan's "long walks" in her healing journey. And it speaks of our steps toward mutual trust and
understanding as we shared in the evolution of this project.

For six months I simply pondered Nan's words. Then I began; first with one
painting, and then several at the same time, in my studio. I adapted a few
of the illustrations from already completed paintings; I found a few that already
fit the verse. All the new paintings were completed in one year of work.

In offering her journey through this book, it was Nan's desire not only to
heal herself but to heal the children and adults of her faith community and,
through this work, to offer healing to the world far beyond Cape Cod.
Nan's daughter, Jennifer, had just arrived home for Thanksgiving break from
college when she became ill. Her parents witnessed her sudden and tragic
death from a rare bacterial infection that affected every organ of her body.
Nan was left with the question: "Where is God in what has happened to
our daughter and us?"

I will never know what it is to lose a daughter. Yet, grief touches us all. For me losing a father at age nine
opened a window into the fragility of life during a time in my life when I was still young and vulnerable.
Art heals by showing us the depths of our lives and our possibilities. Through sharing in Nan's struggle,
I have, as an adult, touched and transformed my own experience of grief. My healing, like Nan's, has
continued one step at a time. These twenty-one paintings are my offering to Nan and to the world.

my daughter died
she was only nineteen
i am very sad

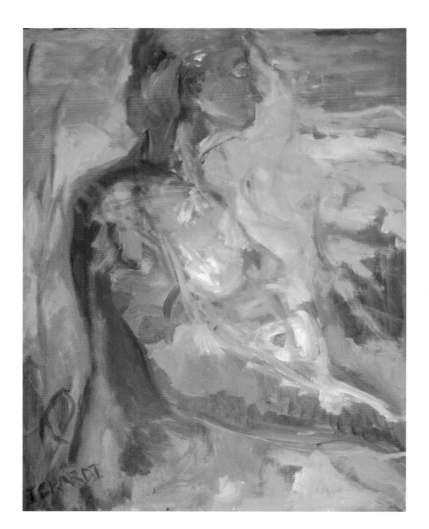

i go for walks in
the winter dusk
where has my jennifer gone?

horse, do you know where
my jennifer is?
no, but you may use my
gentle 'nicker' to remember
her softness

sunset, do you know where
my jennifer is?
no, but you may use my
golden glow to remember her
golden hair

stars, do you know where
my jennifer is?
no, but you may use us
to remember the sparkle in her eyes

candlelight, do you know where
my jennifer is?
no, but you may use my
light in your search

stormy ocean, do you know
where my jennifer is?
no, but you may use my
turbulence and anger to
remind you of her temper
and unhappiness

11

fog, do you know where
my jennifer is?
no, but you may use my
mysteriousness to ask your
questions

dark of night, do you know
where my jennifer is?
no, but you may use me
to hide your tears

rain, do you know where
my jennifer is?
no, but i will cry with you

bird of the morning,
flying high and free
do you know where
my jennifer is?
no, but i will help you
look for her

kitten, do you know
where my jennifer is?
no, but you may use my playfulness
to remember her laughter

sunrise, have you seen
my daughter?
no, but today is a new day
for loving her still

wind, where is my jennifer?
i don't know, but as i blow
through the trees,
remember her singing

baby bird have you
seen my jennifer?
no, but you may use me to
remember your joy
when she was born

crocus, do you know where my jennifer is?
no, but i have been buried
deep in the earth and now i have been set
free to a new life

sun, do you know where
my jennifer is?
no, but i will keep you
both warm

budding tree,
do you know where
my jennifer is?
no, but watch me
change and grow
before your eyes
maybe jennifer has
simply changed and is
still growing too

melting snow, do you
know where my jennifer is?
no, but as i change to water
and trickle away, i'll take
some of your sadness with me

i am still sad
i still take long walks

but somehow i see,
somehow i hear,
somehow i know that
nothing can separate me
from all that jennifer was,
and is,
and will be

Notes on The Paintings

The first painting, "Only Nineteen," voices the darkness and terrible sadness of sudden loss. In dark blues as well as in layers of warm colors, I painted loss and the way it penetrates our bodies and our souls. Like an intense glob of paint, the bereftness is engulfing as pain seeps into all the pores of our being.

"Long Walks" in the winter dusk portrays the growing realization that our loved one is truly gone from this world. The lone orange and yellow figure reflects that sense of nakedness against the soft background of Cape Cod sandy dunes and bright skies. Even in winter, the landscape of the Cape offers soothing gentleness.

"Horse" remains a mysterious creature to me while I so appreciate the intimacy between human and horse. I was inspired by a Christmas card photo of my friend Carleen with her beloved equine companion. I sought to capture how animals console us.

"Sunset" is a view of Hyannisport, not far from the Kennedy compound, a family acquainted with grief.

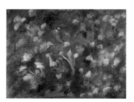

"Stars"sparkle in darkness, like a few moments of memory in a dark sky.

In "Candlelight," abstract shapes and a moving swath of light guide the way in an interplay between the light and purple crosses. Nan and I met during the season of Lent at her church and she died during Lent. In the church of my youth, the cross and holy statues were covered with purple cloth, a sign of Christ's passion. Lent is a time when gradually the darkness is overcome by the light.

The wide brush strokes in "Stormy Ocean" express the turbulence of ocean and the anger of grief as well as the characteristic unhappiness and moodiness of late adolescence.

"Dark of night" was also painted at Provincetown Harbor at low tide after boats had been pulled up on the sand. Back in my studio, I changed the daylight to night. I am intrigued by the shape of boats.

"Bird of the Morning," suggests one of my favorite artists, Marc Chagall. I wanted to capture that freedom to soar like a bird, which keeps hope alive.

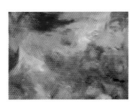

"Sunrise" focuses on soft balmy color, warm yellow and magenta and turquoise. Sunrise reminds us each day we make a choice to keep our love alive.

"Fog" was created at Provincetown Harbor. It was a rainy day and I remember hiding under the wharf for shelter to paint. By heightening the yellow in the sand, I increased the quality of mystery and light.

I painted "Rain" on that same rainy day under the wharf. Back in my studio, I flooded the canvas with cleansing white.

"Kitten" How Nan loved kittens! My own puppy, Duchy, helped me to catch the kitten's playfulness and innocence, qualities Nan and I also reveled in sharing, so healing in the midst of grief.

"Wind" portrays my own English garden that I look out upon first thing every morning from my kitchen window.

Notes on The Paintings *(continued)*

"Baby Bird" rises up like birth, like joy. The higher it goes the lighter it becomes.

I painted "Sun" on a warm glowing spring day. My model was transformed as she leaned against the resplendent reddish purple Japanese tree in the corner of my garden.

"Budding Tree" depicts a magnificent tree that still grows in the backyard where I used to live. After many years, I felt the tree to be blue and I experienced the space around it full with growth and bright colors. Could it be, as Nan and I imagined together, that her daughter, too, was still changing and growing?

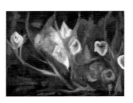

In "Crocus," Nan's favorite painting, living things push through the earth showing us how nature partakes of resurrection. From the depths of our broken hearts, seeds of new life spring.

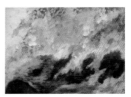

"Melting Snow" is a favorite of mine. It captures the essence of what I tried to accomplish in this series. In this painting, I wanted to render the feeling of melting snow, especially the transformation that begins to carry away the sadness.

In "I still take long walks" darkness still intermingles with light. Each anniversary year remains still difficult, still sad.

"Jennifer." I never met Nan's daughter, Jennifer, but Nan gave me a school picture, which I kept hanging in my studio. I think of this picture as an icon, a holy interpretation of Jennifer's spirit, which, like the love of God, is never separated from all that she is and will be.

To the Reader:
Use this space for your own notes, reflections or poems.

Readers Notes

Readers Notes

Readers Notes

About the Poet

Nanette Geertz inspired many people through her poetry and her calling as a minister. Her first book of poetry, "Journeys" is a moving portrayal of the period of time following her daughter's unexpected death and her own struggle with breast cancer. Nan served as Associate Pastor of the First Congregational Church of Falmouth and as Director of Christian Education at First Church of Christ in Sandwich, Massachusetts. She wrote the prose poem *Walking with Grief* to show people of all ages and faiths ways that the heart and soul heal.

About the Artist

Anne Ierardi's artwork has been shown throughout New England. Anne paints the "landscape of the imagination," aspiring through her art to touch the human spirit in each of us and to awaken what is asleep. Ordained in the United Church of Christ (U.C.C.), Anne expresses her calling through creativity, spiritual direction, and transformational counseling. She is the Director of Healthsigns Center, a nonprofit organization dedicated to fostering wholeness and creativity in the individual and community. She lives in Yarmouthport, Massachusetts with her partner Judy and their mini-poodle Duchy.

Healthsigns Center, Inc. is a nonprofit organization
founded in 1982 dedicated to celebrating creativity,
wisdom, and wholeness in the individual and the community.

For more information or to order copies of *Walking with Grief*
please contact Healthsigns Center, Inc.: 508-375-0700.

Email: amijr@comcast.net
Website: amifinearts.com

Acknowledgments

I am grateful for the support of our friends and colleagues
who believed in this book and for those who provided creative,
technical, and financial assistance. Judith Recknagel, Jane Pearsall,
The Healthsigns Board and the Friends of Healthsigns,
John Clark, Patricia Papernow, John Moore, Beth Silver,
my staff at Healthsigns, and my colleagues in ministry.
-Anne Ierardi